Elle THE HUMANIST

Foreword by
Daniel Dennett

Written by
Elle Harris
and Douglas Harris

Foreword

This is a book of good thinking about important things. Grownups call this kind of thinking philosophy, which comes from ancient Greek words meaning love of wisdom. What this book shows you is that philosophy does not have to be complicated or difficult. Good philosophy just has to be clear and it has to explain whatever it says, so you know the reasons why it is wisdom. One of the important features of this book is that it tries to speak to everyone, no matter what they believe. So it tries to speak to you. Does it succeed? Did you give it a fair chance to succeed? All you have to do is read it carefully and see if you agree. If you don't agree, see if you can say why. Then check your answer and see if it's a good answer, an answer that everyone ought to agree with. If you succeed, you too are a philosopher. Welcome to the club!

Daniel Dennett
University Professor of Philosophy
Tufts University

Hello! My name is Elle

It's nice to meet you!

A humanist is a person who tries to be good because they want to make the world a better place for everyone.

Have you heard of a humanist?

Most of my friends at school haven't, so they ask me questions to understand. Most of the time these questions start when my friends ask me what church I go to.

I tell them that I don't go to any church.

There are many humanist groups that give us the chance to be part of a community—the same way a religious church is a community.

peace and
social justice

EVOLUTION

PHILOSOPHY

BIOLOGY

POETRY 21ST CENTURY

critical thinking

Some humanists choose to be a
part of an organized group.

responsibility

global awareness

environmentalism

JUSTICE
FOR
ALL

TOGETHER

WE'RE
ONE

EQUALITY!

My family's community comes from our friends and family, school and the local soccer club that we love.

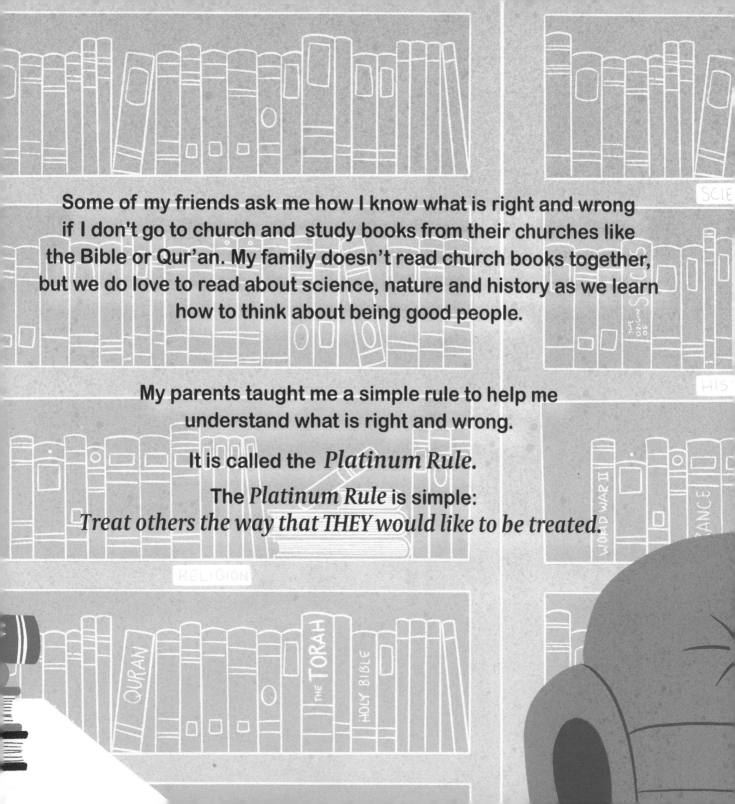

Some of my friends ask me how I know what is right and wrong
if I don't go to church and study books from their churches like
the Bible or Qur'an. My family doesn't read church books together,
but we do love to read about science, nature and history as we learn
how to think about being good people.

My parents taught me a simple rule to help me
understand what is right and wrong.

It is called the *Platinum Rule*.

The *Platinum Rule* is simple:
Treat others the way that THEY would like to be treated.

Rules like this have been taught for thousands of years.

Buddhism:
Treat not others in ways that you yourself would find hurtful.

[Buddha | Udanavarga 5:18 | 6th Century BCE]

Hinduism:
This is the sum of duty:
Do not do to others what would cause pain if done to you.

[Mahabarata 5:1517 | 3rd Century BCE]

Confucianism:
One word which sums up the basis of all good conduct...loving kindness. Do not do to others what you do not want done to yourself.

[Confucius | Analects 15:23 | 3rd Century BCE]

Judaism:
What is hateful to you, do not do to your neighbor. This is the whole Torah; all the rest is commentary.

[Hillel the Elder | Babylonian Talmud, Shabbat 31a:6 | 1st Century BCE]

Christianity:
In everything, do to others as you would have them do to you; for this is the law and the prophets.

[Jesus Christ | Matthew 7:12 | 1st Century CE]

Islam:
Not one of you truly believes until you wish for others what you wish for yourself.

[Muhammad | An-Nawawi's 40 Hadith, No. 13 | 7th Century CE]

You can see on this fun chart
how our *Platinum Rule* is very
much like other Golden Rules.

The humanist version of this, the *Platinum Rule*, is fun and easy.
Here's how I use it:

Would my friend like me to steal her toys?
No! So, I don't steal her toys.

Would my friends like
me to lie to them?

No! So, I don't lie to them.

I can also do nice things with the *Platinum Rule*.
Here's how this works:

Would my friend like me to share
my treats with him?

Would my mom like
me to clean up my
room and help with
the dishes after dinner?

Yes! So, I clean up
my room and help with
the dishes after dinner.

Yes! So, I share my
treats with him.

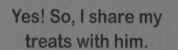

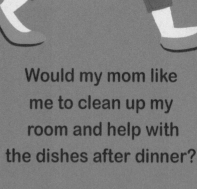

I have to remember that some people don't want to be treated like I want to be treated because we are all very different. This is why the *Platinum Rule* teaches us to treat other people like THEY would like to be treated, not like we would like to be treated.

Here's how this works: I love to be tickled on my feet, but my brother Bryson doesn't like to be tickled on his feet.

So, I don't tickle Bryson on his feet. But I love when my mom tickles my feet.

My friend Brinley doesn't like sushi like I do. So when we have a choice of where to go out to eat, I don't pick sushi restaurants. I try to pick restaurants with pizza because that's Brinley's favorite.

Some of my friends ask me questions like, "How do you know if you're good enough to get into heaven after you die?"

I don't know anything about this, but I know that being a good person and helping others makes the people around me happier, and that this makes me feel happy.

It doesn't matter if you are Chinese, Pakistani, German, Mexican, or if you're from the United States, like me.

Or if you believe in Krishna, Poseidon, Jesus, Muhammad, or you don't believe in any gods or prophets, like me.

We are all trying our best to be happy as
we live on this wonderful Earth.

And being a good person and loving others
makes us all happier than anything else!

Some of our favorite links:

American Humanist Association: www.americanhumanist.org

Humanist Manifesto: www.americanhumanist.org/what-is-humanism/manifesto3/

The Ten Commitments: www.humanistcommitments.org

Effective Altruism: https://www.effectivealtruism.org

Camp Quest: www.campquest.org

Foundation Beyond Belief: https://foundationbeyondbelief.org

Oasis: www.networkoasis.org

Sunday Assembly: www.sundayassembly.com

Unitarian Universalist Association: www.UUA.org

Center For Inquiry: www.centerforinquiry.org

Freedom From Religion Foundation: www.ffrf.org

American Ethical Union: www.aeu.org

Secular Student Alliance: www.secularstudents.org

Skeptic Society: https://www.skeptic.com

Black Non-Believers www.blacknonbelievers.com

Hispanic American Freethinkers: http://hafree.org

Freethought Society: www.ftsociety.org

Friendly Atheist: www.friendlyatheist.patheos.com

Thinking Atheist: www.thethinkingatheist.com

American Atheists: www.atheists.org

Annabelle & Aiden Book Series: www.annabelleandaiden.com

Stardust Book Series: www.stardustscience.com

Society for Humanistic Judaism: www.shj.org

Openly Secular: www.openlysecular.org

Secular Coalition: www.secular.org

Teacher Institute for Evolutionary Science: www.tieseducation.org

Richard Dawkins Foundation: www.richarddawkins.net

Humanists International: www.humanists.international

Humanist Community at Harvard and MIT: http://harvardhumanist.org

Learn more at www.ellethehumanist.com

"Elle's clear, accessible introduction to humanism is perfect for budding freethinkers or any young person who wants to understand how to live well beyond the confines of religious dogma."
–Phil Zuckerman, Ph.D., author of
What It Means to be Moral, Living the Secular Life, and Society without God

his little book about common sense humanism should be available to every questioning youngster."
–Margaret Downey, Founder and President at the Freethought Society

"Elle is for Lovely. This book is lovely!"
–Dan Barker, author of *Mere Morality*

"This is a perfect primer for kids of all ages, helping young humanists navigate the inevitable questions from religious friends."
–Hemant Mehta, editor of *Friendly Atheist*, co-host of *Friendly Atheist Podcast*,
author of *The Young Atheist's Survival Guide*

"This clearly written, concise story offers children being raised without theism a way to share with their friends (of any or no religion) the idea that ethical values of all traditions are ultimately about how people treat one another—a great equalizing message."
–Paul Golin, Executive Director at the Society for Humanistic Judaism

"Elle the Humanist is a wonderful addition to a growing number of children's books on humanism."
–Kristin Wintermute, Director of Education at American Humanist Association

To my wonderful mother, Mackenzie Harris.
E.H.
To Bryson, McKay, Bailey, and Elle.
D.H.
Special thank you to Emily Newman, Education Coordinator at American Humanist Association

LABEL FREE
—PUBLISHING—

Book
Design by
yipjar.com

Printed in the USA
CPSIA information can be obtained
at www.ICGtesting.com
LVHW072133290923
759677LV00069B/63